RICE CAKES

Based on a story from Japan

The Cast:

-  A husband
- A wife
- A chorus of mice

Scene 1

HUSBAND and WIFE are in their kitchen.

Husband: What fine weather! I shall work in our fields all day.

Wife: Then you will need to take some lunch.

Husband: That's a good idea. You can guess what I would like.

Wife: Yes, some delicious rice cakes.

(They put two rice cakes in a container.)

Husband and Wife *(happily):*

Rice cakes, rice cakes.

Two round rice cakes.

Rice cakes make a tasty lunch!

Husband: Good-bye!

(He leaves with his lunch.)

HUSBAND *is in the fields.*

Husband: Mmmm — I'm hungry.

(He reaches for his lunch but knocks it over.)

Oh, no!

(MICE run in.)

Mice *(happily):*

Rice cakes, rice cakes.

Two round *mice* cakes.

Rice cakes make

a tasty lunch!

7

Husband *(puzzled)*: Who is singing? I'm sure I heard something.

Mice: It was us!

Husband: Have you eaten my rice cakes?

Mice: Yes, and thank you!
We were very hungry,
and we *love* rice cakes.

Husband *(sadly)*: So do I —
but now there are none left.

Mice: Don't be sad. We have a special gift for *you*.

(MICE give HUSBAND a small bag. Then they run off.)

Husband *(looking into bag)*: Oh, just a few grains of rice.

Scene 3

HUSBAND arrives back at the house.

Wife: Why are you back so early?

Husband: I dropped the rice cakes
and some mice ate them.
Then they gave me this gift.

(He holds up the bag.)

Wife *(looking in the bag):*
Only a few grains of rice.
Well, that will not make
many rice cakes!

(WIFE starts pouring the rice into a bowl.)

Wife and Husband *(amazed)*: Look — it doesn't stop! The mice have given us a never-ending bag of rice!

(MICE run in.)

Mice: Look at all that rice. Now you will always be able to make rice cakes — and extra ones for us, too!

All: *Rice cakes, rice cakes,*
Nice round rice cakes,
Rice cakes make a tasty lunch.

Rice cakes, rice cakes,
Nice round rice cakes.
Munch, munch, munch,
munch, munch, munch, munch!